Our Words

Dana Barrette

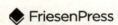

Suite 300 - 990 Fort St
Victoria, BC, V8V 3K2
Canada

www.friesenpress.com

Copyright © 2020 by Dana Barrette
First Edition — 2020

All rights reserved.

No part of this publication may be reproduced in any form, or by any means, electronic or mechanical, including photocopying, recording, or any information browsing, storage, or retrieval system, without permission in writing from FriesenPress.

ISBN
978-1-5255-5883-2 (Hardcover)
978-1-5255-5884-9 (Paperback)
978-1-5255-5885-6 (eBook)

1. POETRY, CANADIAN

Distributed to the trade by The Ingram Book Company

Be still, silence your thoughts
In this moment, creation begins.
All is revealed in a single pause
Listen intently to our words.
Feel the essence of life speak through
A quiet mind brings forth creation
—Dana Barrette

Thank You

Table of Contents

Together 1
We are 3
One 5
The call 7
Thread 9
Cherish 11
All 13
Us 15
Combined 17
As we are 19
Autumn 21
Connected 23
Being 25
Present 27
Rise 29
Create 31
Heedful 33
Receive 35
Summer 37
Aura 39
Time 41
Full 43
Sprout 45
Fruit 47
Path 49
Untitled 51

Key	53
Beauties	55
Creation	57
We are one	59
Through Your eyes	61
Each day	63
Sap	65
Us	67
Source	69
Joy	71
Thank you	73
Glide	75
Trees	77
Expand	79
Harmony	81
Whole	83
Light	85
Sight	87
Food	89
Warmth	91
Serene	93
Awake	95
Unfold	97
Thoughts	99
Observe	101
The talk	103
Winter	105
Hear	107
Awakened	109
Intention	111
Commence	113
Spring	115

Listen 117

Hare 119

Gratitude of heart 121

Sweet. 123

Embrace 125

The door 127

As it be. 129

Gentle 131

Enchanted 133

See 135

Our words 137

Be 139

Passage 141

Circle 143

Sense. 145

Flourish 147

Tears of joy. 149

Grow. 151

Share. 153

Gift 155

Silent chime 157

Pure 159

For Dad 161

Eternal Life 163

Together

11.15.18

As one, we are infinite

As one, abundant

As one, it flows through and expands, all love as is.

Life everlasting, beauty in all, clarity of moments, cherishing as one

The droplets flow down a winter sight, chill in the air, warmth in Your light.

These moments as one, are infinite

Together we are all, together we are

We are

11.19.18

The joy of us, the peace, as one—clarity in all, remembrance of some

Grateful patience, saved by You, now we are all, now we are You

One and the same, forever infinite, beauty in all, the flow of grace

Smooth and dense, it is all as one—infinitely together, infinitely one

One

11.30.18

The flocks they fly, gliding in the wind

Effortless flow, joy to bring

For all to see, for all to receive—a few may see what fullness it brings.

Body of life, warmth of love, energy in all, energy as one

What beauty, together as one.

The call

12.06.18

The energy You bring, the flow of the earth—our eyes are oceans, our ears, the chirping call.

The water flows down our cheeks in gratitude. All is awe.

So many gifts You bring, thankfulness—full, to be one, to feel one, our life complete.

The call You bring—together we will give, for others to see, for others to be.

Thread

12.08.18

The thread, it entwines around us—from us, it flows in the weave

We make the comfort together, we are the makers of peace

All becomes one through gratitude, all becomes one through love

Forever we are infinite, forever we are one

Cherish

12.08.18

A pure heart, we are as one, for eyes to see, glorious love

To touch a hand, to feel the light, magnificent glow, dancing flow

Beauty we are, for all to have, abundant as one, cherishing us

All

12.10.18

As one, we are all

As one, we breathe life

As one, our eyes are kind

As one, our energy flows

As one, our hands are warmth

As one, our hearts are love

As one, gratitude is all

As one, life is complete

As one, we are

Us

12.10.18

This feeling of love, the heart of us, eyes gaze in
wonderment, watching

For all to have and to find—simple answer, gratitude of mind.

Our spirit within, for all to hold, all to feel, and know

Simple as one, beauty of all, one answer known, gratitude of mind.

All will have, all will feel, all will be as us, be as one

Combined

12.11.18

Created by You, essence of all, energy combined, making us You.

Love we are—a sweet smell to the senses, smooth and soft, a blanket of caresses

Always here, always present, forever entwined, forever combined

Gratitude is all.

The heart beats as one, lifting spirits high, forever we are one

As we are

12.12.18

As we are, the trees rooted with us—birds fly, wings of trust

As we are, the tulips bloom, red, yellow, white, May and June

As we are, the rain trickles down, feeling the softness of its plan

As we are, the wind it blows, the energy it brings, endless flow

As we are, the sun warms our skin, renewing us, once again

As we are, the water so deep, creations gliding, in the depths to see

As we are, truth in life, beauty of love, complete

Autumn

12.12.18

Flutter of the leaves, autumn has returned, beautiful sight, colors of patterned trees.

A few hold on to the fall, most surrender to their path, renewing once again, when the time comes to pass.

Although the bareness is great, beautiful wonders can be found, many a birds' nest amongst the view abound.

Intricate detail in all this life, so much joy to see

Fullness in all, our thoughts imagine them to be.

Connected

12.13.18

This knowing inside, as one, intentions clear, awareness bright

Thoughts of beauty, thoughts of love, reveal in us a quiet dove.

So clear and precise, take a look and see, as one—all is revealed, as one—all will be

Joy and awe, our presence gives out, connected to life, connected to us

Come and feel, come and see, all that can be with us

Being

12.14.18

Forever connected, abundant in life, these wonders are formed—appreciation of us

Guiding others, helping their way, relieving the search, as one we stay

Connected through all—life, love, joy, simple truth—us being You

Present

12.15.18

To be awakened by You we have become one—awareness of truth, the joys unfold

The day begins, bringing new light, beautiful sequences, moonlit night.

The flow is present, we see it fly, feeling the moment, endless sky

So much gratitude, so much love, given freely, for all to know

One thought of us, the day is complete, forever together, forever we

Rise

12.16.18

The path is shown, truth unfolds, as one, memories of old

Now is the moment, now is the time, to feel all the love, to have it inside.

Whatever we encounter, we will find

Beauty resides in all, beauty unwinds.

The path is filled with wonders, truths of life

Sip it in your body, feel your inner rise

Create

12.17.18

Time passes, create as one, feelings of us, bringing forth love

Soft as cotton, rough as wool, all are one, time stands still

Flow as one, see the brightness shown, create our piece, together as one.

You will find, great views to be, the awe of *one*, the awe of *we*

Heedful

12.18.18

Ocean waves, repeated flow, time passes, consistent

The day reveals, nature's call, as one we see, as one we are.

Relish in Your love, the life for us, infinite climb, our space as one

Watch the glide, eyes are wide, Your presence.

Tree tops above, looking down, aware of You, aware of us

Life of love, shown in all, true inside, knowing the call.

Receive

12.19.18

In letting go, we receive all that is with us

Calm heart, soft breath, twinkle in our eyes

Effortless flow, warmth within, sparkles in the sky

The sun's heat, the moon's energy, all with us as one

A spider's web, dew on the line, pebbles of sand glimmer—

Feel these joys, sense their love, Creation in us, Creation as one

Summer

12.20.18

Walking through the fields, our hands glide on the golden grass, warm breeze wisps through our fine hair, tickling our neck.

The soft sound of the willows' sway, eyes watch their flow, mind enchanted, thoughts of us, refreshed.

These moments are infinite, always present, as one they remain, as one we stay

Aura

12.24.18

The snow trickles down, peaceful abundance—watching as they float

Softness to the eyes, Your wonders are everything, all that is around us

Soothing to the heart and mind, as one we feel it all

As one it surrounds us, love in all forms, all of us

Time

12.26.18

Feeling us, as one, knowing shown, creative life, warmth of sun, sway of love

As one, we are.

The days are long, the nights short, same in all, everlasting life, life of love, kindness of us

As one, we are.

Cool breeze, moonlit face, strong wind, a summer's end, to return, changes occur

As one, we are.

Full

12.29.18

Love surrounds us—energy inside, sunray's beam, warming our sight

Together we become all that is—joining as one, forever enchanted.

Life so full, we are its brim, flowing unto others—feel the energy within

Radiate our love—as one we are, all there is, eternal life

Sprout

12.30.18

Grateful for us, as one You have shown, the joys of life, the love of all

Seeds they grow, by Your love for them, as one we sprout, entwined within.

Roots grounded, the high trees in sway, graceful motion, one and the same

Awe of life, awe of love, one together, awe of You.

Creation inside, writing out, love for all, to pass on to

Fruit

01.01.19

The bearer of comfort, peace of all, showing strength, from within the call

Creative time, spend our life, one with all, one with You

Joyous wonders, awe of our time, grateful of life

Excited now, these moments of truth, to live as one, being its fruit

Path

01.02.19

Intentions clear, mind at ease—gratitude opens life

The animals watch, we feel their presence, together.

Joyous love, revealing the path, unfolding in front of all—

This is it, the time is now, these moments of love.

Beautiful Love—grateful for You, for us being

Untitled

01.06.19

Blessed with You, Creator of life, one together, this knowing of You

Create our world, bring peace to all, share joys, Your presence the call.

Beautiful wonders, they surround us, loving in others, their light
is shown

Thankful for You, gratitude great, to live this life, abundant in You.

Experiencing awe, in all things, this life our love

Key

01.09.19

Right now, all around us—look into the essence of life:

Wind blowing, fluttering wings, their presence, joy in all things.

Life's creation lives inside us. Becoming one, you heed your call

Life everlasting, part of natural flow. Feel your love, your connection with all.

You will find the peace it brings, tranquil waters diving into springs

True love for all to know—gratitude, the key to it all

Beauties

01.09.19

Trickling snow, flowing, softness felt inside, thoughts flow to us, graciously abide

Gently caress the tree tops, birds flying in our path, true beauty found in watching, mesmerized

One with us, one with You, beauties unfold

Life to be just as is, all with You

Creation

01.10.19

Infinity of all, together as one, grateful love, creative expanse

Journey of joy, caress of time, infinitely one, love of life

Teacher of peace, Being of warmth, tears of thankfulness, for all we are one

Gathering moments, releasing away, enjoy the newness, expanding our sway

Blessed with You, to be as one

We are one

01.11.19

We are one—the wind carrying us

We are one—rays of sun illuminating life

We are one—solid oak roots woven in earth

We are one—trickling waters of salty blue sea

We are one—beating heart of flying wonders

We are one—grass so green tickling our feet

We are one—the eyes stare, minds connected

We are one—magnetic moon, flowing energy

We are one—flakes of snow, glittering light

We are one—golden leaves, autumn's embrace

We are one—love connects humanity in peace

We are one—Love

Through Your eyes

01.13.19

Watching through Your eyes, life is bright—luminous clouds, trees of light

Shimmering grass glows in the sway, running waters, endless array.

Watching through Your eyes, tall beauties shine—leaves of golden green, sun's warmth, yellow and blue, a gentle haze.

Watching through Your eyes—energy flowing, birds relishing all moments, enjoying their flight.

Beauty through Your eyes, beauty as one

Each day

01.14.19

Traveling together through this beautiful world, encountering love from all of You

Peaceful senses, joyful minds brought to us, gathered by You.

Birds they soar high above, giving us lessons to hear, watch, energies combined, soothing sounds to the ear.

This love of abundance, tranquility so great, bringing smiles day after day—

Thank you, gratitude pure, for us being as one

Sap

01.15.19

Ground to roots the tree is formed, energy inside, its flower the essence of all

Calling to us, the bare branches reach to the sky, wonderment known, the beauty held within.

Fullness in its bareness from the energy it gives, relish in its giving the sap of life

Coarse bark holds it firmly from the elements, thriving by the essence of life.

Soft leaves of warm glow, eyes in wonderment cherish, passing through, feeling energy from all, calmness of life, balanced

Us

01.15.19

Energy of life, Creator of love, essence of all, one with You

Abundance of peace, beautiful expression, receptive to all, one with You

Kind warmth, expanding time, loving to all, one with You

Life as motion, flowing vines, simple measure, one with You

Clouds building, sun a blaze, warming us, one with You

Grateful life, tranquil love, blessings abound, one with You

Source

01.16.19

Soft flow, brilliant light, energy source, essence of life
Strong winds, branches sing, grounded together by You.
Calling out, for us to come, enjoy the moment, as one
Receptive to all, life everlasting, answering the call
For You are life, core as one, beauty found, in all

Joy

01.21.19

Love—endless ray of light

Patience—soft water permeating rocks

Creation—energy flowing to and from

Abundance—stars' bright timeless glow

Kind—silky smooth tulip in bloom

Receptive—all can be as one with You

Beautiful—cherish the trees in all their form

Expanding—consistent change to renew, rebirth

Gratitude—immense joy with You

Thank you

01.23.19

Thank you for love—bountiful expression

Thank you for patience—swirling around till sight has come

Thank you for energy—feelings awakened

Thank you for time—moment to moment

Thank you for life—Creation's wonders

Thank you for creativity—our mind combined

Thank you for flow—our essence aligned

Thank you for breath—to share our words

Thank you for us—complete

Glide

01.30.19

Creation—breath of life, energy of all

Gratitude—patience, expanding unto appreciation

Knowledge—watching, kindness to us

Flowing—beautiful, warmth of touch

Abundant—everlasting, thirst is quenched

Beautiful—combined, life everlasting

Trees

01.31.19

Graciously here, infinite, love shown, the trees,

Hearts warmed, rays of sun, clouds up high, a winter's tale,

Water trickling, quenched thirst, birds of wonder, a sparrow's song,

Quiet laughter, dancing squirrels, magnetic pull, full moon bright,

Snow glistening, sparkling light, energy soars, our life

Expand

02.03.19

Let us go beyond our thoughts, feeling our love, soaring through the streets, flight into our conscious dreams.

Expand our energy to feed the world, help them know peace

Commence their journey with You, revealing their inner glee

This life with You, this life as us, immeasurable time

Truth, love and beyond, connected

Harmony

02.05.19

Deep into our conscious, deep into our heart, Your energy can be found, and brought forth into our life.

It attracts all our wishes, it attracts all our dreams, to be at one with You, peaceful calmness for all to see.

Our energy combined, with all of life, essence entwined, we feel love

Love of our Creator, love for all things, in complete harmony we sing

Whole

02.7-8.19

Energy permeates our skin, spirit aligned

As one we soar high

As one we revel in the cold

As one all is beauty

As one we are whole.

To walk in grace with You, Creator of all, intention's light

Every day listening to You, morning till night, dreaming of truth

To live a life with energy from all, Your creations—infinite, giving forth love

Signs of calling flow through time, patience growing, gratitude of life.

Enchanted by wonders all around, thoughts of life abound

Glorious snow flowing about, trees surround, abundant in sight.

Light

02.10.19

Inner peace, gentle caress, hand in hand, vibration flows,

Healing commence, soft and light, flowing in waves, energy,

Together we are pure, together love, life of abundance, energies one,

Creating our world, our time to soar, tranquil moments, light brought forth,

Motions infinite, travelling within, each moment, joy seen

Sight

02.13.19

Thick, dense snow, ice topped trees, winter's warm glow, nightly sight to see

Great wonders are seen through Your eyes, take a look and feel, flowing energy climb

Through our toes, to our heavy minds, bringing forth peace, calmness inside

Revel in all Creation, through Creation's eyes, to be as one, energy glides

Gratitude for life brings love in all, a life of abundance, pure

Food

02.16.19

Hearing the call, us as one, create for others, feel our love,

The love all have, inside with You, to continue in time, bringing forth truth,

This love is brought when we truly feel good, appreciating Your presence, appreciating Your food,

Food of the mind, food for the heart, energies connected, creating our force,

A force to heal, and be healed inside, as one we flourish, as one we provide,

To help our friends, to connect the world, peace as one

Warmth

02.18.19

Can you feel it? Permeate your skin, feeling oneness, Creation within

Blanket of silk, wrapped around, warmth of energy, absorbed.

Through this oneness truth be told, others are listening, ready,

To tell their story, creativity be

All is as one

Serene

02.19.19

Tingling senses, breathing light, heartbeat calm, surrounded by light

In a space, together one, free and clear, silence found

Pure energy, blissful moment, peaceful feeling, light as one

Awake

02.21.19

Feeling of love—light and bright, free motion, soaring high

Creative together—us as one, words clear, awakened mind

Ask in love—aura surrounds, energy magnifies, wishes found

Always consistent, present in all moments, joys in all treasures, brought by You

Quiet reflection, feeling Your love, adoring moments, this life with You

Unfold

02.22.19

Elements of love protect us, surrounded by peace of mind

Life lived, attracting all, desires and passions combined.

Passion brings forth our creative mind, teaching unto others, through words

Feeling their purpose, all will be revealed.

Tapping into your essence, thankfulness felt

Renewing of your inner self, reveals life, through time.

Truth be told, calmness inside, all brought forth by You

Creator of all, truth of life, Love.

Thoughts

02.23.19

Signs brought forth, reveal our path—observe as they come to pass

Appreciation is all you need, for your Creator inside,

Marvels and delights will be brought forth, formed by creative thought

Joys of life, awe of wonder flow unto your being,

Awakened at the core, energies glowing,

True to life, to your Creator, blissful harmony

Observe

02.24.19

Connected—beauty of grace

Forever—surrounded by love

Essence—coming forth, truth of life

Awakened—observing time

Joy—gratitude for all received

Love—peace connected

As all—our Creator

Universal mind—our source of life

The talk

02.25.19

Clear the mind, cleanse the soul, inner life, peace be told

Graceful love, abundant in all, gratitude calls, wonderment of You.

Always here, truth of life, our presence together, creative mind

Soar through consciousness, memories past, future kind, our moment told,

Through these words, now with all, glorious peace

Winter

02.26.19

Warm, bright sun travels through the clouds, day is cold, a winter's snow, trees dreaming are still,

Birds soar, flowing with You, their presence known, living life as You,

Slow drifts catch the eye, abundant energy flows,

Graceful movement of all things, peaceful love divine

Hear

02.28.19

Always present, beautiful love—calm inside, energy bright—flowing,

Light, airy wind—connected—part of You

Together time stands still—graceful moments—love is—create now

Our words expressed—release us to hear

Expand together, peace known

Awakened

03.01.19

Mind is clear, love be told, love as all, joy

Ocean sky, movement seen, we build our nest, words woven,

Spring into joy, spring into us, energy as one, our life, complete.

Hand in hand, heart in heart, bring to others creative parts,

To feel Your love, abundance known, pass on to others, expand our glow

May they know You, Creator of life, all is kind through Your eyes.

Intention

03.01.19

This is where life begins, creativity of mind

Deep in your being, appreciation of You, intention bearer of truth

To revel in these delights each day, moments are endless

Feelings bright, Creation in you, brings forth love, calling you to be

Commence

03.03.19

Slow beat, energy raised, love formed, aura of light

Gentle vibration, expanding thoughts, higher level, conscious light

Into life, into love, hold their truth, create their love

Worlds together, hearts entwined, earth of peace, energies combined

To us as one, to be for all, commence, create, show forth love

Spring

03.05.19

Deep breathe, light air, flowing grace, heart to heart

Many wonders, life be told, through our energies, together whole,

Sweet blossoms, coming forth, spring balances out the old

Memories to come, our future foreseen

Words of life, now spoken

Listen

03.06.19

Thoughts emerge, deep silence, listen intently, quiet whisper

Open your ears, to hear your call, create with intention, all is love

Peace given, for all who see, wondrous feeling, our energies be

At one with all, Creation's delight, heeding your call, everlasting life

Hare

03.08.19

Healing mind, healing heart, soft whispers, swift in thought
Words of love, words of beauty, continuum.
Peaceful warmth, abundant touch, tranquil life, as us.
Lovely hare, sensing my stares, ears listening, silent.
Grateful time is all moments, sameness felt, Love.

Gratitude of heart

03.09.19

Open your heart to all that be, together we create our words,

Guided in thought, mind and heart, through this world of life.

To feel and see the wonders around, peace builds into our time,

Glide together through the trees, joyfully combined.

Beautiful colors, abundance of light, all wonders to adore

One thought to bring these moments, gratitude of heart,

Hence our love is shared, for others to read and feel

Your light rises in their hearts, their purpose revealed.

Sweet

03.13.19

Every wisp of wind tickling our skin, joyful energy beaming within

Truth in nature, all love found, Your presence, silent, beautiful sound.

Sweet glide, our friend of air, circling about, sensing Your stare

Moments together, energy combined, all is present, peace of mind.

Fluttering about, sweet butterfly love, colors unique, delicate pause

Creation's beauties, for all to feel and sense. Life is revealed.

Our time, to create, to be entwined, joyful love, peace of time

Embrace

03.14.19

Glowing with life, energies soar, truth be told, brilliant light

New moments transpire, creativity flows, into our words.

Share with all who want to feel, to see and touch the energy, heal

We are as is, life core, centre wheel, infinitely us.

This life embraced by You, kind measure, spirit of truth

Peace surrounds, unity all, energy high, love of all

Create together, be the will—intention clear, mind still.

The door

03.15.19

Knock, knock, open door, swiftly come and see

Salty air, ocean blue, light summer breeze

Flow together, soar up high, endless flight

Through time, moments now, cherishing light

Be as one, be as all, forever infinite

Travel far, travel near, beginning clear

Gratitude flows, to and through, hands hold

Quiet silence, tranquil ear, lovely sound of us

Whispering wind, blowing life, infinite space,

Lovely life, timeless place, together grace

As it be

03.16.19

To think of our love infinitely, words they be whole, one as love can describe, the simple truth of it all.

Passing moments, energies flow, to and from, aligned, attract us, we sense peace, eyes to eyes, calm.

The wish of thoughts, thoughts become our future untold, what we perceive, see it be, through our eyes of love.

All will reveal their energies now. Watch, enjoy our soar, combined infinitely, embraced at the core.

We are all as it be, Your creation so bright, abundant in love, abundant in life

To be graceful love, water deep, stingrays sense, energies meet

Silver blue, our future be, all from You.

Gentle

03.18.19

Whispering wind guides our path, gentle flow, skin to skin

Warm water, gentle breeze, together, forever ease

Light flutter, airy ride, moment to moment, continuous glide

Love of You, love as one, infinitely close, infinitely us

Enchanted

03.20.19

Slow breath, grateful silence, energies calm, together

Life wondrous, calm heart, beating, new, silent.

Tingling presence, relaxing thought, mind at ease, life

Sweet sound, sparrows' song, curious time, enchanted.

Time great, life flow, words placed, create

Follow now, time be, us together, life.

See

03.22.19

Ask to receive all you seek, glorious life be

For all who cherish love, love from their Creator see

Our intention will guide us, guide us to be

All, to everyone around us, all who seek to see,

Light shines upon us, mirrored by our inner bright

Abundance reveals in us, answers to our wishes in life

Gratitude for our love, our connection to our words

Peace among those who chose their path,

Come all who thirst, for our time to create

To be at one with our Creator, brings Creation to all who seek

Our words

03.23.19

Now, this moment, time for us, create our words, write our thoughts

Give to others, cherish belief, marvel in life, peace it be

Steps taken, shown in all ways, it permeates, our space

Infinitely bound, circle of grace, love found, tender embrace

Let all be, as is, pure joy

Be

03.24.19

Allow our light to shine, be the wind's whisper, all to see and watch, one together

Life is ours, create our words to pass, time is now, illuminated stance

Energy permeates, new our moments, peace flourishes, giving to all

As they are, Creation's will, be.

Passage

03.26.19

The bud it grows, blossoming moonlight, energy flows to and from

Creation's breath, giving life, the splendor, kindness shown

Our world becomes clear, thoughts will bring, life's desires dear

Our heart combined, where energy flows, Creation as one, our eyes glow

For all to witness, our transition to life, eternal shape, our eternal guide

Circle

03.27.19

Circle of love, circle of life, we flow, round and round

Morning dew, brilliant sky, moonlit blue, love of life

Pure joy, waking now, energy high, sun so bright

Thankfulness be, all of You, gratitude now, beliefs of truth

To be together, heart as one, spread our peace, create our love

Sense

03.30.19

Hearing Your call, flow with You, belief now, love truth

Abundance in all, light to guide, gratitude of heart, now combined

Quiet sense, extraordinary life, life together, our words

Time to create, feel our joy, sense our peace, life uncoils

Flourish

03.31.19

To release our energies, thoughts given, kindness to others.
Life forms.

Through our appreciation, our future now, others can feel, our persistent flow

What can we give, to live in love? Give freely, abundance will show.

Many forms brought, only one can be, true and divine, the Creator of thee

Access our intention, gratitude inside, all will flourish, abundant life

Tears of joy

03.31.19

Glorious life, energy, flow of grace, watching
Pause in time, moments, beauty resides in all.
Sun shining, divine light, salty stream, gratitude
Love, infinite, create, our words.

Grow

04.01.19

Be mindful of your thoughts, they bring about the truth, your future will be, all you see,

Hear your call, take action and grow, all your wishes met, all your desires told,

Can you feel it now? It shall come, enjoy our time, infinite life

Share

04.02.19

Connected with You, life brings, graceful moments, peace within

To be combined, our thoughts bring about, our present call to give in life

Our words, grateful mind, grateful heart, energies aligned

The path shown, to be at one, peace for all, share our love

Gift

04.02.19

Mind free, in the moment, cool breeze, sense the wind

Feel each beat, beat of our heart, breathing slowly, our moment within

Hearing Your voice, gift for all, gratitude pure, reveals our call

Be now, forever dear, mind and heart, intention clear

Silent chime

04.03.19

Flash of light, soothing peace, calmness felt inside,

No thoughts remain, pure bliss, our moment still,

Sense of water, floating about, free of time,

Still, quiet, unplugged clock, hearing nothing chime.

All is love, creative, in between thoughts,

Burst of energy, come forth, creation begins

Pure

04.04.19

Pause, there it is, the moment, pure energy, blissful light, joy

One divine mind, our Creator, our Love

All possible, from this moment, aligned. All flows.

For Dad

04.05.19

To be as we are, waking to beauty, sunrise glows each morning, thoughts of our day

Bring our future, our life, aligned; our day is bright

Combined, peace flows, grateful for us, eternal love

Eternal Life

04.05.19

To create

our joy

To share

our words

To see

all as is

To be

aligned, full

To love

peace

To cherish

gratitude

To speak

words true

To sense

energies flow

You are

Eternal Life

Printed in the USA
CPSIA information can be obtained
at www.ICGtesting.com
LVHW041531271023
762201LV00014B/1803